Domestic
Monastery

Domestic
Monastery

RONALD
ROLHEISER

PARACLETE PRESS

Brewster, Massachusetts

2019 First Printing

Domestic Monastery

Copyright © 2019 by Ronald Rolheiser
Cover image copyright © 2019 by Brother Michael O'Neill McGrath, osfs

ISBN 978-1-64060-372-1

Library of Congress Cataloging-in-Publication data is available.

10 9 8 7 6 5 4 3 2 1

Published by Paraclete Press
Brewster, Massachusetts | www.paracletepress.com

Printed in Korea

CONTENTS

ONE

Monasticism *and* Family Life

There is a tradition, strong among spiritual writers, that we will not advance within the spiritual life unless we pray at least an hour a day privately. I was stressing this one day in a talk, when a lady asked how this might apply to her, given that she was home with young children who demanded her total attention.

"Where would I ever find an uninterrupted hour each day?" she moaned. "I would, I am afraid, be praying with children screaming and tugging at my pant legs."

A few years ago, I might have been tempted to point out to her that if her life was that hectic then she, of all people, needed time daily away from her children, for private prayer, among other things. As it is, I gave her different advice: "If you are home alone with small children whose needs give you little uninterrupted time, then you don't need an hour of private prayer daily. Raising small children, if it is done with love and generosity, will do for you exactly what private prayer does."

Left unqualified, that is a dangerous statement. It, in fact, suggests that raising children is a functional substitute for prayer.

However, in making the assertion that a certain service—in this case, raising children—can in fact be prayer, I am bolstered by the testimony of contemplatives themselves. Carlo Carretto, one of the twentieth century's best spiritual writers, spent many years in the Sahara Desert by himself praying. Yet he once confessed that he felt that his mother, who spent nearly thirty years raising children, was much more contemplative than he was, and less selfish. If that is true, and Carretto suggests that it is, the conclusion we should draw is not that there was anything wrong with his long hours of solitude in the desert, but that there was something very right about the years his mother lived an interrupted life amid the noise and demands of small children.

St. John of the Cross, in speaking about the very essence of the contemplative life, writes: "But they, O my God and my life, will see and experience your mild touch, who withdraw from the world and become mild, bringing the mild into harmony with the mild, thus enabling themselves to experience and enjoy you" (*The Living Flame*, 2.17).

In this statement, John suggests that there are two elements crucial to the contemplative's experience of

"But they,
O my God and my life,
will see and experience
your mild touch,
who withdraw
from the world and
become mild,
bringing the mild into
harmony with the mild,
thus enabling themselves
to experience
and enjoy you"

— St. John of the Cross

12 • Domestic Monastery

God—namely, withdrawal from the world, and the bringing of oneself into harmony with the mild. Although his writings were intended primarily for monks and contemplative nuns who physically withdraw from the world so as to seek a deeper empathy with it, his principles are just as true for those who cannot withdraw physically.

Certain vocations—for example, raising children— offer a perfect setting for living a contemplative life. They provide a desert for reflection, a real monastery. The mother who stays home with small children experiences a very real withdrawal from the world. Her existence is certainly monastic. Her tasks and preoccupations remove her from the centers of social life and from the centers of important power. She feels removed.

Moreover, her constant contact with young children, the mildest of the mild, gives her a privileged opportunity to be in harmony with the mild and learn empathy and unselfishness. Perhaps more so even than the monk or the minister of the gospel, she is forced, almost against her will, to mature. For years, while she is raising small children, her time is not her own, her own needs have to be put into second place, and every time she turns around some hand is reaching out demanding something. Years of this will mature most anyone. It is because of this that she does not need, during this time, to pray for an hour a day. And it is precisely because of this that the rest of us, who do not have constant contact with small children, need to pray privately daily.

We, to a large extent, do not have to withdraw. We can, often, put our own needs first. We can claim some of our own time. We do not work with what is mild. Our worlds are professional, adult, cold, and untender. Outside of prayer, we run a tremendous risk of becoming selfish and bringing ourselves into harmony with what is untender. Monks and contemplative nuns withdraw from the world to try to become less selfish, more tender, and more in harmony with the mild. To achieve this, they pray for long hours in solitude.

Mothers with young children are offered the identical privilege: withdrawal, solitude, the mild. But they do not need the long hours of private prayer—the demands and mildness of the very young are a functional substitute.

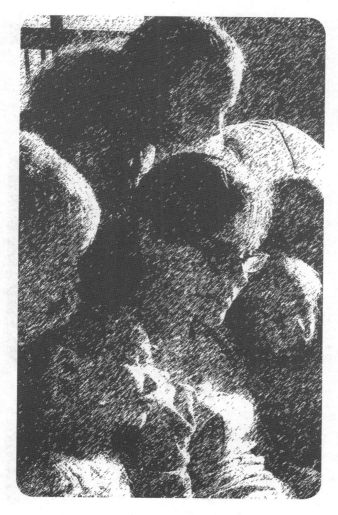

Monasticism *and* Family Life • 15

TWO

The Domestic Monastery

L et's return to Carlo Carretto, that terrific spiritual writer of the past half century, who lived for more than a dozen years as a hermit in the Sahara Desert. Alone, with only the Blessed Sacrament for company, milking a goat for his food, and translating the Bible into the local Bedouin language, he prayed for long hours by himself. But when he returned to his native Italy one day to visit his mother, he came to that startling realization mentioned in chapter 1: His mother, who for more than thirty years had been so busy raising a family that she scarcely had a private minute for herself, was more contemplative than he was.

Carretto, though, was careful to draw the right lesson from this. What this taught was not that there was anything wrong with what he had been doing in living as a hermit. The lesson was rather that there was something wonderfully right about what his mother had been doing all these years as she lived the interrupted life amidst the noise and incessant demands of small children. He had been in a monastery, but so had she.

What is a monastery? A monastery is not so much a place set apart for monks and nuns as it is a place set apart, period. It is also a place to learn the value of powerlessness and a place to learn that time is not ours, but God's.

Just like a monastery, our home and our duties can teach us those things. The vocation of monastic monks and nuns is to physically withdraw from the world. But the principle is equally valid for those of us who cannot go off to monasteries and become monks and nuns. Certain vocations offer the same kind of opportunity for contemplation. They too provide a desert for reflection.

St. Bernard, one of the great architects of monasticism, used to refer to the "monastic bell." All monasteries have a bell. Bernard, in writing his rules for monasticism, told his monks that whenever the monastic bell rang, they were to drop whatever they were doing and go immediately to the particular activity (prayer, meals, work, study, sleep) to which the bell was summoning them. He was adamant that they respond immediately, stating that if they were writing a letter they were to stop in mid-sentence when the bell rang. The idea in his mind was that when the bell called, it called you to the next task and you were to respond immediately, not because you want to, but

because it's time for that task and time isn't your time, it's God's time. For him, the monastic bell was intended as a discipline to stretch the heart by always taking you beyond your own agenda to God's agenda.

So, let's return again to Carlo Carretto's mother. Any mother or father, while raising children, perhaps in a more privileged way even than a professional contemplative, is forced, almost against the will, to constantly stretch the heart. For years, while raising children, her or his time is never her or his own. Personal needs have to be kept in second place, and every time a parent turns around a hand is reaching out and demanding something. A parent hears the monastic bell many times during the day and has to drop things in mid-sentence and respond, not because they want to, but because it's time for that activity and time isn't one's own, but God's.

The rest of us experience the monastic bell each morning when our alarm clock rings and we get out of bed and ready ourselves for the day, not because we want to, but because it's time.

22 • Domestic Monastery

What is a monastery?
A monastery is not so much
a place set apart for monks and nuns
as it is a place set apart,
period.

The principles of monasticism are time-tested, saint-sanctioned, and altogether trustworthy. But there are different kinds of monasteries, different ways of putting ourselves into harmony with the mild, and different kinds of monastic bells. Response to duty can be monastic prayer, a needy hand can be a monastic bell, and working without status and power can constitute a withdrawal into a monastery where God can meet us. This is one simple and ordinary way that the domestic can be the monastic.

THREE

Real Friendship

It was the Cistercian monastic fathers of the twelfth century who wrote memorably about friendship: how the friendship between human beings can reflect and inspire greater friendship between a person and God. But there is nothing privileged about friendship in monastic life. For any of us, in any kind of domestic and everyday life, one of the richest experiences of grace that we can have this side of eternity is the experience of friendship.

Dictionaries define *friendship* as a relationship of mutual affection, a bond richer than mere association. They then go on to link *friendship* to a number of words: *kindness*, *love*, *sympathy*, *empathy*, *honesty*, *altruism*, *loyalty*, *understanding*, *compassion*, *comfort*, and (not least) *trust*. Friends, the dictionaries assert, enjoy each other's company, express their feelings to each other, and make mistakes without fear of judgment from the other.

That basically covers things, but to better grasp the real grace in friendship a number of things inside that definition need explication.

First, as the Greek Stoics affirmed, and as is evident throughout Christian spirituality, true friendship is only possible among people who are practicing virtue. A gang is not a circle of friendship, nor are many ideological circles. Why? Because friendship needs to bring grace, and grace is only found in virtue.

Next, friendship is more than merely human, though it is wonderfully human. When it is genuine, friendship is nothing less than a participation in the flow of life and love that's inside of God. Scripture tells us that God is love, but the word it uses for love in this case is the Greek word *agape*, a term that might be rendered as "family," "community," or "the sharing of life." Hence the famous text "God is Love" might be transliterated to read: God is family, God is community, God is shared existence, and whoever shares his or her existence inside community and friendship is participating in the very flow of life and love that is inside the Trinity.

But this isn't always true. Friendship and family can take different forms. The contemporary Quaker writer Parker Palmer submits: "If you come here faithfully, you bring great blessing."

Conversely, the great Sufi mystic Rumi writes: "If you are here unfaithfully, you bring great harm." Family and community can bring grace or block it. Our circle can be one of love and grace, or it can be a one of hatred and sin. Only the former merits the name *friendship*. Friendship, says St. Augustine, is the beauty of the soul.

Deep, life-giving friendship, as we all know, is as difficult as it is rare. Why? We all long for it in the depths of our soul, so why is it so difficult to find? We all know why: We're different from each other, unique, and rightly cautious as to whom we give entry into our soul. And so it isn't easy to find a soulmate, to have that kind of affinity and trust. Nor is it easy to sustain a friendship once we have found one.

Sustained friendship takes hard commitment, and that's not our strong point as our psyches and our world forever shift and turn. Moreover, today, virtual friendships don't always translate into real friendships.

Finally, not least, friendship is often hindered or derailed by sex and sexual tension. This is simply a fact of nature and a fact within our culture and all other cultures. Sex and sexuality, while they ideally should be the basis for deep friendship, often are the major hindrance to

"The end of friendship
  may be more important
  than love.
The epiphanies of youth
are meant to blossom
and ripen into
something everlasting."

—MICHEL DE MONTAIGNE

30 • Domestic Monastery

friendship. Moreover, in our own culture (whose ethos prizes sex over friendship), friendship is often seen as a substitute, and a second-best one at that, for sex.

But while that may be in our cultural ethos, it's clearly not what's deepest in our souls. There we long for something that's ultimately deeper than sex—or that is sex in a fuller flowering. There's a deep desire in us all (be that a deeper form of sexual desire or a desire for something that's beyond sex) for a soulmate, for someone to sleep with morally. More deeply than we ache for a sexual partner, we ache for a moral partner, though these desires aren't mutually exclusive, just hard to combine.

Friendship, like love, is always partly a mystery, something beyond us. It's a struggle in all cultures. Part of this is simply our humanity. The pearl of great price (from Jesus's profound parable in Matthew's Gospel, chapter 13) is not easily found nor easily retained. True friendship is an eschatological thing, found, though never perfectly, in this life. Cultural and religious factors always work against friendship, as does the omnipresence of sexual tension.

Sometimes poets can reach where academics cannot, and so I offer these insights from a poet vis-à-vis the interrelationship between friendship and sex.

Friendship, Rainer Marie Rilke suggests, is often one of the great taboos within a culture, but it remains always the endgame: "In a deep, felicitous love between two people you can eventually become the loving protectors of each other's solitude. . . . Sex is, admittedly, very powerful, but no matter how powerful, beautiful and wondrous it may be, if you become the loving protectors of each other's solitude, love gradually turns to friendship."

And as Michel de Montaigne affirmed in one of his classic essays: "The end of friendship may be more important than love. The epiphanies of youth are meant to blossom and ripen into something everlasting."

Real Friendship • 33

FOUR

Lessons *from* the Monastic Cell

ere's some advice from the Desert Fathers and Mothers: Go to your cell, and your cell will teach you everything you need to know. Here's another counsel from Thomas à Kempis's famous book *The Imitation of Christ*: Every time you leave your cell you come back less a person.

On the surface, these counsels are directed at monks, and cell refers to the private room of a monk, with its small single cot, its single chair, its writing desk, its small basin or sink, and its kneeler. The counsels suggest that there is a lot to be learned by staying inside that space, and there are real dangers in stepping outside it. What can this possibly say to someone who is not a monk or contemplative nun?

These counsels were written for monks, but the deep principles underlying them can be extrapolated to shed wisdom on everyone's life.

What's the deep wisdom here? These counsels are not saying, as has sometimes been taught, that a monastic vocation is superior to a lay vocation. Nor are they saying that, if someone is a monk or a professional contemplative, social interaction outside one's cell is unhealthy.

36 • Domestic Monastery

Cell, as referred to here, is a metaphor, an image, a place inside life, rather than someone's private bedroom. Cell refers to duty, vocation, and commitment. In essence, this is what's being said:

Go to your cell, and your cell will teach you everything you need to know: Stay inside your vocation, inside your commitments, inside your legitimate conscriptive duties, inside your church, inside your family, and they will teach you where life is found and what love means. Be faithful to your commitments, and what you are ultimately looking for will be found there.

Every time you leave your cell you come back less a person: This is telling us that every time we step outside our commitments, every time we are unfaithful, every time we walk away from what we should legitimately be doing, we come back less a person for that betrayal.

There's a rich spirituality in these principles: Stay inside your commitments, be faithful, your place of work is a seminary, your work is a sacrament, your family is a monastery, your home is a sanctuary. Stay inside them, don't betray them, learn what they are teaching you without constantly looking for life elsewhere and without constantly believing that God is elsewhere.

"There's a rich spirituality
in these principles:
Stay inside your commitments,
be faithful,
your place of work is a seminary,
your work is a sacrament,
your family is a monastery,
your home is a sanctuary.

What we have committed ourselves to constitutes our monastic cell. When we are faithful to that, namely, to the duties that come to us from our personal relationships and our place of work, we learn life's lessons by osmosis. Conversely, whenever we betray our commitments as they pertain to our relationships or to our work, we become less than what we are.

We are all monks, and it matters not whether we are in a monastery or are in the world as spouses, parents, friends, ministers in the church, teachers, doctors, nurses, laborers, artisans, social workers, bankers, economic advisors, salespersons, politicians, lawyers, mental health workers, contractors, or retirees. Each of us has our cell, and that cell can teach us what we need to know.

FIVE

Ritual *for* Sustaining Prayer

In a homily at a wedding, Dietrich Bonhoeffer once gave this advice to a young couple: "Today you are young and very much in love and you think that your love can sustain your marriage. It can't. Let your marriage sustain your love."

Love and prayer work the same: The neophyte's mistake is to think that they can be sustained simply through good feelings and good intentions, without the help of a ritual-container and a sustaining rhythm. That's naïve, however sincere. Love and prayer can only be sustained through ritual, routine, and rhythm. Why?

St. John of the Cross says what eventually makes us stop praying is simple boredom, tiredness, lack of energy. It's hard, very hard, existentially impossible, to crank up the energy, day in and day out, to pray with real affectivity, real feeling, and real heart. We simply cannot sustain that kind of energy and enthusiasm. We're human beings, limited in our energies, and chronically too tired, dissipated, and torn in various directions to sustain prayer on the basis of feelings. We need something else to help us. What?

Ritual—a rhythm, a routine.

42 • Domestic Monastery

Monks have secrets worth knowing, and anyone who has ever been to a monastery knows that monks (who pray often and a lot) sustain themselves in prayer not through feeling, variety, or creativity, but through ritual, rhythm, and routine. Monastic prayer is simple, often rote, has a clear durational expectancy, and is structured to allow each monk the freedom to invest himself or hold back, in terms of energy and heart, depending upon his disposition on a given day. That's wise anthropology.

Prayer is like eating.

There needs to be a good rhythm between big banquets (high celebration, high aesthetics, lots of time, proper formality) and the everyday family supper (simple, no-frills, short, predictable). A family that tries to eat every meal as if it were a banquet soon finds that most of its members are looking for an excuse to be absent. With good reason. Everyone needs to eat every day, but nobody has energy for a banquet every day. The same holds true for prayer. One wonders whether the huge drop-off of people who used to attend church services daily isn't connected to this. People attended daily services more when those services were short, routine, and predictable, and gave them the freedom to be as present or absent (in terms of emotional investment) as their energy and heart allowed on that given day.

Today, unfortunately, we are misled by a number of misconceptions about prayer and liturgy.

Too commonly, we accept the following set of axioms as wise: Creativity and variety are always good. Every prayer celebration should be one of high energy. Longer is better than shorter. Either you should pray with feeling or you shouldn't pray at all. Ritual is meaningless unless we are emotionally invested in it.

Each of these axioms is overly romantic, ill thought out, anthropologically naïve, and unhelpful in sustaining a life of prayer. Prayer is a relationship, a long-term one, and lives by those rules. Relating to anyone long-term has its ups and downs. Nobody can be interesting all the time, sustain high energy all the time, or fully invest himself or herself all the time. Never travel with anyone who expects you to be interesting, lively, and emotionally invested all the time. Real life doesn't work that way. Neither does prayer.

What sustains a relationship long-term is ritual, routine, a regular rhythm that incarnates the commitment.

Imagine you have an aged mother in a nursing home and you've committed yourself to visiting her twice a week. How do you sustain yourself in this? Not by feeling, energy, or emotion, but by commitment, routine, and ritual. You go to visit her at a given time, not because you feel like it, but because it's time. You go to visit her in spite of the fact that you sometimes don't feel like it, that you sometimes can't give her the best of your heart, and that often you are tired, distracted, restless, overburdened, and are occasionally sneaking a glance at your watch and wondering how soon you can make a graceful exit.

Moreover, your conversation with her will not always be deep or about meaningful things. Occasionally, there will be emotional satisfaction and the sense that something important was shared, but many times, perhaps most often, there will only be the sense that it was good that you were there and that an important, life-giving connection has been nurtured and sustained, despite what seemingly occurred at the surface. You've been with your mother, and that's more important than whatever feelings or conversation might have taken place on a given day.

Prayer works the same way. That's why the saints and the great spiritual writers have always said that there is only one nonnegotiable rule for prayer: "Show up! Show up regularly!" The ups and downs of our minds and hearts are of secondary importance.

"There is only one
nonnegotiable rule for prayer:
"Show up!
Show up regularly!"
The ups and downs
of our minds and hearts
are of secondary importance.

SIX

Tensions *Within* Spirituality

Healthy spirituality has always been a question of putting a number of things into delicate balance and then walking a tightrope so as not to fall off either side. Spiritual health is very much the task of living the proper tension between a number of things:

1) The tension between contemplation and action: How much of our lives should be given over to action and how much to prayer? What is the essence of religion? Private prayer and private morality? Or service to others and social justice? What ultimately will save the planet—soul craft or statecraft? This tension is often depicted as the one that is described in the biblical passage of Martha and Mary. Martha engaged herself in the necessary task of serving others while Mary simply sat at Jesus's feet, doing nothing, but loving a lot. Jesus commends Mary, saying she has chosen the better part. Christian spirituality forever after has had to struggle with those words. Is prayer really more important than active service?

The saints would have us do both. A healthy spirituality is not a question of choosing between Mary and Martha, but of choosing both—contemplation and action, soul craft and statecraft, loving and doing, prayer and service, private morality and social justice.

2) The tension between the monastic and the domestic: Where is God most easily found—in the church or in the kitchen? In the monastery or in the family? In a celibate monk's cot or in the marriage bed? At a shrine or in a sports stadium? The God we believe in is both the holy God of transcendence and the incarnate God of immanence. God is, in a privileged way, found in both the monastic and the domestic, the church and the world. A healthy spiritual life keeps a robust respect for both.

3) The tension between passion and purity: What is the secret for depth in sexuality, passion, or purity? What ultimately brings us a soulmate—eros or awe? Again, the saints would say it is both. Sexuality will only surrender its real depth and arouse its singular power to unite when it is surrounded with both the fire of passion and the reticence of purity.

4) The tension between duty and personal actualization: What ultimately is the higher call, duty or personal fulfillment? Are we in this world called to serve others or to exercise fully the talents that God has put into us? Which call to us is the higher moral imperative— that which comes from family, church, and country or that which comes from those centers within us that ache for the personal in love, art, achievement, and immortality? Again, if the saints can be believed, it is a question of both, of balance, of walking a tightrope, of living a daily tension.

5) The tension between this life and the next: What is more important, this world or the next? Within what perspective do I make decisions—the span of my years here on earth or the horizon of eternity? How much potential happiness should I sacrifice here in this world in view of eternal life? Is this life a vale of tears or a valley of opportunity? The Christian view is that both are important. When Jesus said, "I have come so that you may have life," he was referring both to life after death and life after birth.

6) The tension between intellect and will: What is more important—the head or the heart? By which should we guide our lives? What should be the ultimate basis for our decisions, thought or feelings? What is more valuable, insight or love? The wisdom of the saints suggests that a healthy spiritual life, not to mention a full humanity, demands both—head and heart, thought and feelings, the rational and the emotional.

7) The tension between community and individuality: Are we in this world primarily to fulfill a personal vocation, or is our primary purpose a communitarian one? Might an individual's personal freedom be sacrificed for the good of the group? Or should the common good be less important than personal freedom? Again, a healthy spiritual life walks the proper tension between these polarities. It refuses to sacrifice the individual for the group even as it asserts that we are essentially communitarian and that we have nonnegotiable obligations toward community.

Contemplation and action, the monastic and the domestic, passion and purity, duty and self-actualization, this life and the next, intellect and will, community and individuality . . . all of these, like a complete set of keys on a piano, are needed if we hope to play all the tunes that the various circumstances of our lives demand. One is wise not to cut off part of one's keyboard.

54 • Domestic Monastery

Contemplation and action,
the monastic and the domestic,
passion and purity,
duty and self-actualization,
this life and the next,
intellect and will,
community and individuality . . .
all of these, like a complete set of
keys on a piano, are needed if we
hope to play all the tunes that the
various circumstances of our lives
demand. One is wise not to cut
off part of one's keyboard.

SEVEN

A Spirituality
of Parenting

As we saw in the example of Carlo Carretto's realization about the depth of his mother's spirituality (see chapter 1), Christian theology has generally been weak in its treatise on everyday faithful domestic living. Somehow the earthiness of the incarnation, so evident elsewhere, has been slow to spill over into our thinking about marriage, sex, and family.

There are reasons for this, of course, among them the fact that often those writing the books on marriage are themselves not married, but celibate monks and nuns. There are other issues, as well. In the early church, the influence of Manichaeanism (a dualistic view of the world that pitted "light" against "darkness" and presumed whatever was of this earth and life to be evil or bad) made the church somewhat reticent to genuinely celebrate the goodness of sex and marriage; and, later on, the monastic ideal (of celibate life outside marriage) came to be so identified with holiness that marriage, sex, and parenting were not seen as having within them the same inherent, privileged path to sanctity as celibacy and the monastic life.

Monastic life was seen as a "higher state," an elite path to holiness not available to anyone married. Granted, there was always a theology that taught that one's duties of state, such as the demands inherent in parenting, were a certain compulsory path to holiness, but, in the end, this didn't add up to a full, wholesome theology of marriage, sex, and parenting.

More than twenty years ago now, at a conference in Collegeville, Minnesota, I heard a talk given by Dr. Wendy Wright, a mother and theologian.[1] She spoke wonderfully of a spirituality of parenting. In essence, she suggested that raising children, being a mom or a dad, is a privileged means to holiness and—this is my addition—a more natural path to maturity than is to be found in monasticism. Simply put, very few other experiences, perhaps none, are as naturally geared to break the casings of our inherent selfishness as is the experience of child-raising. (This brings us back to Carretto's experience.)

---

[1] She's written many important books. I refer you to these two, for instance: *Seasons of a Family's Life: Cultivating the Contemplative Spirit at Home*, and *Sacred Dwelling: Discovering and Living Your Family Spirituality*.

To be a mother
or a father
is to let your dreams
and agenda
be forever altered.

A flexible heart
is a discerning heart;
it picks up each moment
and discerns the true
and the false voices within it.
It asks, in each moment,
"Where does love lie
for my child in all this?"

To see your own child is to feel what God must feel when God looks at us. Parenting, in the end, is the most natural path to holiness and maturity, what often feels like a compulsory commitment, and takes us where we would often rather not go. Becoming a parent, submits Dr. Wright, reshapes the heart in a unique way, molding it more and more to be compassionate as God is compassionate. Here are some of her thoughts:

Being a mother or a father stretches the heart, just as the womb is stretched in pregnancy. This is because, among all loves, parental love is perhaps the one that most pulls your heart out of its self-love. Parenting reshapes the core of your being to help you to love more like God loves.

Seeing your own child's fragility and morality works to create in you feelings of inexpressible tenderness that help you feel what God must feel when God looks at us. To be a parent is to be formed in a school of love.

The Trappist monk and spiritual writer Michael Casey, ocso, once wrote—using this traditional phrase for monastic life—"the monastery is a school of love because it teaches us to forget ambition, convenience and self-gratification in order to open our hearts to love." Is there an aspect of our lives where this could be truer to reality than in the everyday, domestic lives of parents with small children?

One of the first lessons this school of love teaches you is welcome: To be a parent is to have to permanently open your heart, life, and plans so as to create a unique space in them for someone else, your child. To be a mother or a father is to let your dreams and agenda be forever altered.

The next lesson this school of love teaches is flexibility: To be a parent is to nurture a child as he or she passes through very different stages of growth: infancy, toddlerhood, kindergarten, elementary school, a teen with raging hormones and a raging attitude, a young adult, an adult with his or her own responsibilities and unique sorrows. Moreover, if you have more than one child, each has a unique personality that you must adapt your love toward. All of this demands that you constantly grow, re-adjust, adapt, let go, learn to love in a new way.

A flexible heart is a discerning heart; it picks up each moment and discerns the true and the false voices within it. It asks, in each moment, "Where does love lie for my child in all this?" This is a demanding task for a parent, one within which, as Wright so well puts it, "looking good is not the point!"

A parent must ever say
in word and attitude,
"Return as far as you can
and I will come
the rest of the way."

Finally, being a parent should naturally lead you to shape your heart for reconciliation. Love is all about forgiving, again and again and again. Families survive only if this is happening. A parent is meant to be the compassion of God, the father and mother of the prodigal son and the bitter brother, who embraces the child not because the child is worthy, but in spite of all unworthiness. A parent must ever say in word and attitude, "Return as far as you can and I will come the rest of the way."

All these things can, of course, be done by anyone, not just biological parents. However, for a mom or a dad, there is a certain naturalness in it, a conscriptive rhythm written by nature itself. To be a parent is to find oneself enrolled in an elite school of love, a true monastery that is every bit as ascetical and grace-producing as any monastery ever praised by the great spiritual writers.

EIGHT

Spirituality *and* the Seasons *of* Our Lives

As a young man, Nikos Kazantzakis, the famous twentieth-century Greek writer (*Zorba the Greek*; *Christ Recrucified*; etc.), contemplated becoming a monk and once spent a summer touring monasteries. Years later, writing on the experience, he recounted a marvelous conversation he had with an elderly monk, Fr. Makarios.

At one point, he asked the old monk: "Do you still wrestle with the devil, Father Makarios?" The old priest sighed and replied: "Not any longer, my child. I have grown old now, and he has grown old with me. He doesn't have the strength. . . . I wrestle with God." "With God!" Kazantzakis exclaimed in astonishment. "And you hope to win?" "I hope to lose, my child," the old man replied. "My bones remain with me still, and they continue to resist."

Among other things, this story highlights the fact that our spiritual struggles change as we age and go through life. The struggles of youth are not necessarily the struggles of midlife and beyond. Maturity is developmental. Different things are asked of us as we move through life. This is also true for spirituality and discipleship.

How does our spiritual life change and demand new things from us as we grow? Drawing upon the insights of St. John of the Cross, I would submit that there are three fundamental stages to our spiritual lives, three levels of discipleship:

The first level, which John of the Cross calls the "dark night of the senses," might aptly be called Essential Discipleship. In essence, this is the struggle to get our lives together. This struggle begins really at birth but becomes more our own individual struggle when we reach puberty and begin to be driven by powerful inner forces to separate ourselves from our families so as to create a life and a home of our own. During this time, we struggle to find ourselves, to get our lives together, to create a new home for ourselves. This can take years and might never be achieved. Indeed, for most everyone, some elements of this struggle will continue throughout their entire lifetime.

But, for most people, there comes a time when this is essentially achieved, when there is a sense of being at home again, when the major questions of life are no longer:

Who am I?

What will I do with my life?

Who loves me?

Who will marry me?
Where should I live?
What should I do?

At some point, most of us find a place beyond these questions: We have a home, a career, a marriage partner or some peace without one, a vocation, a meaning, a good reason to get up every morning, and a place to return to at night. We have found our way home again.

We then enter the second level of discipleship, which John of the Cross calls "proficiency" and which we might call Generative Discipleship. In essence, this is the struggle to give our lives away. Our main concern now is not so much about what to do with our lives but how to give them away so as to make the world a better place. These are our generative years, and they are meant to stretch from the time we land in a vocation, a career, and a home, until our retirement years. And our major questions during these years need to be altruistic ones:

How do I give myself over more generously and more purely?

How do I remain faithful?

How do I sustain myself in my commitments?

How do I give my life away?

72 • Domestic Monastery

But those are not yet the ultimate questions: At some point, if we are blessed with health and life beyond retirement, a still deeper question begins to arise in us, one that invites us to a third stage of discipleship. As Henri Nouwen used to say: At a certain point in our lives the question is no longer: What can I still do so that my life makes a contribution? But, how can I now live so that when I die, my death will be an optimal blessing to my family, the church, and the world?

John of the Cross calls this stage the "dark night of the spirit." We might call it Radical Discipleship, because at this stage we are not so much struggling with how to give our lives away but with how to give our deaths away. Our questions now become:

How do live the last years of my life so that when I die my death will bless my loved ones just as my life once did?

How do I live out my remaining years so that when I die "blood and water" will, metaphorically, flow from my dead body as they once flowed from Jesus's dead body?

Too little within our spiritualities challenges us to look at this last stage of life: How do we die for others? However, as Goethe puts it in his poem "The Holy Longing," life itself will eventually force us to contemplate whether we want to become "insane for the light."

NINE

The Sacredness
of Time

Brother David Steindl-Rast once commented that leisure is not the privilege of those who have time, but rather the virtue of those who give to each instant of life the time it deserves. That's a valuable insight, especially today when everywhere life seems dominated by the constraints of time.

Always, it seems, there isn't enough time. Our lives are dominated by pressure, the rat race, demands that are all-absorbing. The manufacturing plant has to run and, by the time that is taken care of, there is no time or energy for anything else.

And we are conscious of our pathological busyness. We know that life is passing us by, and we are so preoccupied with the business of making a living and the duties of family and community that only rarely is there any time to actually live. It seems that there is never any unpressured time, unhurried time, undesignated time, leisure time, time to smell the flowers, time to simply luxuriate in being alive. We lament about this over our coffee circles but are unable to effectively change anything. Is there something frighteningly wrong with our lives? Is there a need to drastically change our lifestyles?

Perhaps. Obviously in our lives there is too little family time, prayer time, celebration time, and simply restful time. But we are also compounding our problem through misunderstanding. Philosophies of "taking time to smell the flowers" have sometimes led us to understand leisure precisely as the privilege of the rich and unoccupied.

What Steindl-Rast challenges us to do is to understand time correctly. Time is a gift. When T. S. Eliot says, "Time, not our time," he is pointing out that there needs to be a certain detachment from time, a certain monasticism, in our lives.

Monks and nuns know that time is not their own, that they must often drop whatever they are doing and move on to what is being asked of them next. When the bell rings, St. Benedict once said, the monk must put down his pen without crossing his *t* or dotting his *i*. He must move on, not necessarily because he feels like doing something else, but because it is time . . . time to eat, or pray, or work, or study, or sleep.

Monks' lives are regulated by a bell, not because they don't have watches and alarm clocks, but to remind them, always, that time is not their own and that there is a proper time to do things. Monks don't get to sleep, eat, pray, work, or relax when they feel like it, but when it's time to do those things.

There is an astonishing parallel between that and what happens in our own lives, and we can be helped by understanding it. There is an inbuilt monasticism to our lives. At least for the more active years of our lives, we too are called to practice a certain asceticism regarding time— to have our lives regulated by "the bell."

In our case, it takes a different form, though its demands are the same. In our case, it is an alarm clock and the dictates of our daily lives: a quick breakfast, a commute to work (carrying a bag lunch), staying home with small children, demands at work or at home, driving kids for lessons, dealing with them and their demands, household chores, cooking, laundry, taking out garbage, calling in a plumber, church on Sundays. Like monks we sleep, rise, eat, pray, and work, not necessarily when we'd like to, but when it's time.

This is true not just for our daily routine, but as well for the seasons of our lives. We go to school, we prepare for a career, we enter the workforce, we are tied down with kids, mortgage payments, car payments, and the demands of family and work, not necessarily because we always feel

80 • Domestic Monastery

" Leisure is not the privilege
of those who have time,
but rather the virtue of those
who give to each instant of
life the time it deserves."

–Br. David Steindl-Rast

like it, but because it's that time in our lives. The play of children and the leisure of retirement come before and after that season.

During all the most active years of our lives we are reminded daily, sometimes hourly, that time is not our own; we are monks practicing a demanding asceticism. There will not always be time to smell the flowers, and we are not always poorer for that fact. Monasticism has its own spiritual payoffs. To be forced to work, to be tied down with duties, to have to get up early, to have little time to call your own, to be burdened with the responsibility of children and the demands of debts and mortgages, to go to bed exhausted after a working day is to be in touch with our humanity. It is too an opportunity to recognize that time is not our own and that any mature spirituality makes a distinction between the season of work and the Sabbath, the sabbatical, the time of unpressured time.

Most important of all, recognizing in our duties and pressures the sound of the monastic bell actually helps us to smell the flowers, to give to each instant of our lives the time it deserves—and not necessarily the time I feel like giving it. We are better for the demands that the duties of our state in life put on us, despite constant fatigue. Conversely, the privileged who have all the time in the world are worse off for that, despite their constant opportunity to smell the flowers. These are monastic secrets worth knowing.

TEN

Life's
Key Question

Several years ago, while on retreat, an elderly monk shared with me about the ups and downs of fifty years of monastic life. At the end of this he said to me: "Give me some hints on how I should prepare to die! What should I do to make myself more ready for death?"

The heaviness of such a question is enough to intimidate a person with a spirituality deeper than my own, and when it's asked by someone twice your age whose heart seems already deeply charitable, faith-filled, and wonderfully mellowed through years of quiet prayer, then perhaps the best answer is silence. I wasn't so naïve as to offer him much by way of an answer, his trust in me notwithstanding.

But it's a good question. How do we prepare to die? How do we live so that death does not catch us unawares? What do we do so that we don't leave this world with too much unfinished business?

The first thing that needs to be said is that anything we do to prepare for death should not be morbid or be something that distances or separates us from life and each other. We don't prepare for death by withdrawing from life. The opposite is true. What prepares us for death, anoints us for it, in Christ's phrase, is a deeper, more intimate, fuller entry into life. We get ready for death by beginning to live our lives as we should have been living them all along. How do we do that?

The theologian and storyteller John Shea once suggested that the kingdom of heaven is open to all who are willing to sit down with all. That's a one-line caption for discipleship. In essence, the single condition for going to heaven is to have the kind of heart and the kind of openness that makes it possible for us to sit down with absolutely anyone and to share life and a table with him or her. If that is true, then the best way we can prepare to die is to begin to stretch our hearts to love ever wider and wider, to begin to love in a way that takes us beyond the natural narrowness and discrimination that exists within our hearts because of temperament, wound, timidity, ignorance, selfishness, race, gender, religion, circumstance, and our place in history.

We prepare to die by pushing ourselves to love less narrowly. In that sense, readying ourselves for death is really an ever-widening entry into life.

John Powell, in his book *Unconditional Love*, tells the story of a young student who was dying of cancer. In the final stages of his illness, he came to see Powell and said something to this effect:

Father, you once told us something in class that has made it easier for me to die young. You said: "There are only two potential tragedies in life, and dying young isn't one of them. These are the two tragedies: If you go through life and don't love and if you go through life and you don't tell those whom you love that you love them."

When the doctors told me that my cancer was terminal, I realized how much I've been loved. I've been able to tell my family and others how much they mean to me. I've expressed love. People ask me: "What's it like being twenty-four years old and dying?" I tell them: "It's not so bad. It beats being fifty years old and having no values!"

We prepare ourselves for death by loving deeply and by expressing love, appreciation, and gratitude to each other. Jesus says as much. When the woman at Bethany poured an entire bottle of expensive ointment on his feet and dried his feet with her hair (see Matthew 26, Mark 14, and John 12), he commented on her lavish expression of affection and gratitude by saying: "She has anointed me for my impending death." What he meant should not be piously misinterpreted. He wasn't saying: "Since I'm soon to die, let her waste this ointment!" He was saying rather: "When I come to die, it's going to be easier because, at this moment, I am truly tasting life. It's easier to die when one has been, even for a moment, fully alive."

What makes it difficult for us to die, beyond all the congenital instincts inside of us that want us to live, is not so much fear of the afterlife or even fear that there might not be an afterlife. What makes it hard to die is that we have so much life yet to finish and we finish it by loving more deeply and expressing our love more freely.

Had that old monk cornered Jesus and asked him the same question he asked me, I suspect Jesus might have said:

Prepare for death by living more fully now.

Work at loving more deeply, less discriminately, more affectionately, and more gratefully.

Tell those close to you that you love them and death will never catch you like a thief in the night.

ABOUT THE AUTHOR

RONALD ROLHEISER, OMI, is a specialist in the fields of spirituality and systematic theology. His regular column in the *Catholic Herald* is featured in newspapers in five different countries. He is the author of many books, including bestsellers such as *The Holy Longing*, *Sacred Fire*, also *The Restless Heart*, *Forgotten Amongst the Lilies*, and *Bruised and Wounded*. He lives in San Antonio, Texas, where he is president of the Oblate School of Theology.

ABOUT PARACLETE PRESS

WHO WE ARE

As the publishing arm of the Community of Jesus, Paraclete Press presents a full expression of Christian belief and practice—from Catholic to Evangelical, from Protestant to Orthodox, reflecting the ecumenical charism of the Community and its dedication to sacred music, the fine arts, and the written word. We publish books, recordings, sheet music, and video/DVDs that nourish the vibrant life of the church and its people.

WHAT WE ARE DOING

BOOKS | PARACLETE PRESS BOOKS show the richness and depth of what it means to be Christian. While Benedictine spirituality is at the heart of who we are and all that we do, our books reflect the Christian experience across many cultures, time periods, and houses of worship.

We have many series, including *Paraclete Essentials*; *Paraclete Fiction*; *Paraclete Poetry*; *Paraclete Giants*; and for children and adults, *All God's Creatures*, books about animals and faith; and *San Damiano Books*, focusing on Franciscan spirituality. Others include *Voices from the Monastery* (men and women monastics writing about living a spiritual life today), *Active Prayer*, and new for young readers: *The Pope's Cat*. We also specialize in gift books for children on the occasions of Baptism and First Communion, as well as other important times in a child's life, and books that bring creativity and liveliness to any adult spiritual life.

The MOUNT TABOR BOOKS series focuses on the arts and literature as well as liturgical worship and spirituality; it was created in conjunction with the Mount Tabor Ecumenical Centre for Art and Spirituality in Barga, Italy.

MUSIC | The PARACLETE RECORDINGS label represents the internationally acclaimed choir *Gloriæ Dei Cantores*, the *Gloriæ Dei Cantores Schola*, and the other instrumental artists of the *Arts Empowering Life Foundation*.

Paraclete Press is the exclusive North American distributor for the Gregorian chant recordings from St. Peter's Abbey in Solesmes, France. Paraclete also carries all of the Solesmes chant publications for Mass and the Divine Office, as well as their academic research publications.

In addition, PARACLETE PRESS SHEET MUSIC publishes the work of today's finest composers of sacred choral music, annually reviewing over 1,000 works and releasing between 40 and 60 works for both choir and organ.

VIDEO | Our video/DVDs offer spiritual help, healing, and biblical guidance for a broad range of life issues including grief and loss, marriage, forgiveness, facing death, understanding suicide, bullying, addictions, Alzheimer's, and Christian formation.

Learn more about us at our website:
www.paracletepress.com
or phone us toll-free at 1.800.451.5006

YOU MAY ALSO BE INTERESTED IN . . .

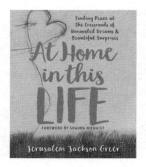

At Home in this Life

Finding Peace at the Crossroads
of Unraveled Dreams and
Beautiful Surprises

Jerusalem Jackson Greer

ISBN 978-1-61261-632-2 | $18.99

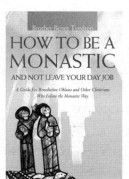

How to Be a Monastic and Not Leave Your Day Job

A Guide for Benedictine Oblates
and Other Christians Who Follow
the Monastic Way

Br. Benet Tvedten

ISBN 978-1-61261-414-4 | $15.99